Inertia: A Study

poems by

Melissa Helton

Finishing Line Press
Georgetown, Kentucky

Inertia: A Study

For Keith, whose love is the force that broke my inertia.
For Kelsey and Violet, whom I love bigger than the sky.

Copyright © 2016 by Melissa Helton
ISBN 978-1-63534-031-0 First Edition
All rights reserved under International and Pan-American Copyright Conventions. No part of this book may be reproduced in any manner whatsoever without written permission from the publisher, except in the case of brief quotations embodied in critical articles and reviews.

ACKNOWLEDGMENTS

Dam was published in *Rivet Journal*
Epithalamium was published in *The Notebook: a progressive journal about women & girls with rural & small town roots*
Ghost Dad Goes Antique Shopping with Me was published in *Pine Mountain Sand and Gravel*
Gravidity was published in *Motif v. 4. Seeking its Own Level: Writings about Water*
Hog Killing in Deep Snow was awarded 2nd prize George Scarborough Poetry Prize, Lincoln Memorial University Mountain Heritage Literary Festival
Last To-Do Lists was published in *Kudzu*
Lazarus's Alarm Clock, Ossified and The Women's Gown were published in *Still: The Journal*
Ossified was Judge's Choice 2014 for poetry

I would like to give special thanks to some of the many people who have shown me support and encouragement, and have offered opportunity and invaluable feedback including Darnell Arnoult, Marianne Worthington, Thomas Alan Holmes, Lars Thacker, and Savannah Sipple. Also, thanks to Southeast KY Community & Technical College for the ability to attend workshops where many of these poems were born.

Publisher: Leah Maines

Editor: Christen Kincaid

Cover Art: D. Keith Helton

Author Photo: Kelsey Pearl Helton

Cover Design: Elizabeth Maines

Printed in the USA on acid-free paper.
Order online: www.finishinglinepress.com
also available on amazon.com

Author inquiries and mail orders:
Finishing Line Press
P. O. Box 1626
Georgetown, Kentucky 40324
U. S. A.

Table of Contents

Potential

Watchings 1
An Astronaut's Perfect Day 2
Crossing Between, in Three Parts 3
Gravidity 4
Waiting 5
Encephalitis 6
Half-Life 8
The Dying Emperor 9

External Force

Lazarus's Alarm Clock 10
To Speak So They Can Hear You 11
Things We Should Chart the Energy of 12
Erythrophobia 13
Eating Flowers 14
Night Falls on the House of Animals 15
Encountering the Only 16
Caul 17
Ghost Dad Sings Birdcalls 18

Acceleration

Athena to Zeus 19
Aerophobia 20
Hog Killing in Deep Snow 21
I Touched My Father's Ashes 24
Images for Grief 25

Momentum

The Women's Gown 26
We Don't Waste Flat Land on the Dead 27
What She Cannot Lay Down 28
Epithalamium 29
Nephophobia 31
Hospice 32

Equal & Opposite Reaction

Last To-Do Lists 35
Ghost Dad Goes Antique Shopping with Me 36
Dam 37
Ossified 38

Potential

Watchings

I watch the field of dandelions
and mandarin poppies. He's speaking
of winterfeed for hummingbirds.
*No food out after Labor Day,
they have to know to move on. If you look after them,
they won't migrate.*
I'm only a girl, not even firstborn
and he cradled me, a yowling pigeon,
like a soft gray dwarf star.

And I read today about the Egyptian hippo-goddess Ta-uret,
a hippo with breasts, guarding
royal women in childbirth.
The river horse, ham-fisted,
water feculent with hay and footprints the size of a child
ushering in and blessing royalty.
I trace in the book,
the immodest hippo dancing,
the water plants, reeds and fronds. I know

she's a decoy really, like bridesmaids
to distract the devil,
or a locomotive's cowcatcher, there to deflect
the ugly, the stupid, the clumsy,
keep the baby from being a useless turnip,
bald cypress. I was that girl
born in the room grandmother died in,
the circumference of it a pentecostal screaming,
midwife's hands like octopuses,
squirming in the olive and sod-red ink of birth.
That girlchild, a gulch, an acid ravine
cut by a torrent. A new Pangaea
to separate.

*See them dart? Their wings sound
like a hailstorm over the cornfields.*

An Astronaut's Perfect Day

Out in the thin, eternal black, stars still as small
as they are from the fields of the Midwest,
I float, a bright human-shaped satellite, tethered
by an umbilical cord to science's womb. Out in this,

    the airless mind of god, I float

like his thought before he pointed and separated
the heavens and the waters. No up. No down. No inside.
Only out—a breath exhaled here would expand,
molecules spreading to chase after all

    the charging corners of the universe,

out where physical laws and uncompromising silence
can terrorize the human into believing in god, and that we,
so special, are something—

    I float.

Crossing Between, in Three Parts

I.
This is the kind of cold air that dries the throat
without apology.
Membranes tighten and cause the voice to shrink
and crack, allowing unintended tilts and nuances
to stowaway, hitch a ride. You can't do much to prevent it.
The cold is coming from the core of everything around you.

II.
The green glass lantern looks so alive
when holding a sunbeam, passive in the day.
But when lit, it projects plasma and photons,
throws a sickness over everything.
It is a light that looks mean.

II.a.
The ghost moth flirts with the glass, asking for consent to enter
which will not come. I can't imagine
if its little ghost moth brain is full of hope
or frustration, or nothing, but it pecks
its question over and over and the glass says no.
I wonder if they know what is at stake.

II.b.
We all have our own holy rituals.

III.
Joints grind, internal creaking, like memories that won't cease
if we are awake. They should be quiet, private, hidden, but sometimes,
the people walking next to us can hear them.

Gravidity

—so much like gravity the sound
of weight, of solid mass, and sliding forces,
fluid trickling down through bedrock vein into a secret—
so much like a woman with her rift
and blood aquifer to fill with water in the dark.

To ask a man to give you a child is irrevocable
and scouring, a slow feeling of grains flayed
by a steady drip, hand on the divot between
hip bone peaks. An immediacy leaches
into that vein—minerals from a pea-sized gland.

I've asked him to fill the dark with fluttering noise,
and the water table rises, postponed.

Waiting

I.
A bristled cedar shoulders up and out two inches this growing season beside the flashing rush of interstate.

The 18-year cycle of moon millimeters over in purple sky from one end of the yard to the other, year after year, only to resign and return.

Faded barn collapsed over, slat boards missing, last year's milkweed stalks scratch a window edge. The ground digests the ruin.

A heavy bundle tires one hip and creaking shoulders
rest it on the other.

Small green flashes in the grass, slower and fading. The firefly's pulses: tally marks in the dark night.

Along the railroad tracks, chalky rocks spill from between the ties
into the field like hatchling leatherbacks, barreling for the blue salt waves.

II.
It seems the only perpetual living condition.

Particles gather, combine,
accumulate in bone, first
dimpling youthful cartilage,
then yellowing enamel.

Constant bombardment from the stars, passing through
like radio waves,
like cultural fear,
like god.
Celestial residue brushes against the cells,
spinning them like Tibetan prayer wheels.

And they wait in their spinning.
To begin.
To end.
To change.

Always for something other
than the light in which we sit
growing older.

Encephalitis

He stares like that red tail hawk
at the clinic. She had West Nile
and swayed on her perch,
eyes glazed—
he will react when you shout,
snap his face toward you,
but blurs through, not really seeing.
I can't stand it.
Turn on the TV so his eyes
can stare elsewhere.
The Yankees.
He doesn't like baseball—
better than infomercials though,
wrinkle vanisher,
vacuum-packed sweaters
in stiff bags like giant rainbow beef jerky.
The stare makes me seasick.
Go to the ICU waiting room,
magazine with Amazing Summer Rhubarb Recipes—
it's March and gray
roads edged in dirty snow.
Scrawled list of foreign doctor names,
short-infectious-disease-lady, neurologist-man-with-the-limp.
Warm grapes, flat 7-UP.
Kitty puzzle.
Game show clang.
Cramped neck.
Hot Pinesol cloud.
Hushed phone calls in the corner.
Guy's wife has lupus and bacterial meningitis.
She died.
Woman's father, a heart attack.
He died too.
Glossy squeak of magazines,
gritty eyelids,
fitful nap,
children running to the vending machines.
Yellow tissue globs.
Someone's pastor sits on my couch,
visitors bring more magazines.
Phone call phone call phone call.
Should I go in and
see him? He's sleeping,
or staring.
ICU= Idiots Carrying Umbrellas.

= Iconoclastic Catholic Underwear.
= Innards Can't Unclench.
= I Crave Ukuleles.
= Icelandic Chocolate Udders.

I cry unnoticing—
drips on crosswords,
flinches if I touch him.
His eyes look, but through me.
I'm a ghost.
He didn't know my name when I drove him here.
By the third spinal tap he couldn't talk.
Repeat the story,
tell another clipboard.
Help the nurse roll him to change his diaper,
my husband's diaper.
He kept pulling out the catheter
before he stopped moving—
now just the stare.
Tell another phone receiver
four days now.
I sit in there when he sleeps,
eyes mercifully closed,
but not with that false awake.
I can't stand it.
Go look out the window.
Get up.
Look, the flat soapy river,
open drawbridge,
rusty freighter laboring
in the dredged channel.
How deep is the channel?
Just imagine if the freighter crashed
into the bridge abutment,
the magnificent rubble.

Half-Life

The math of my father's children tangles:
five by birth but seven he raised,
and four by marriage,
one he never knew,
and I am the last—who can't answer
How many brothers and sisters do you have?

      The one he says is most like him.

I feel this presence in our bones—
the radioactive flecks of him defining
cells as daughter elements,
created not from action, but from decay,
taking years to break down like uranium,
half-life of 4.5 billion years,
the age of the earth.

      How long will it take?

And I am left, deep inside
rock, a mile back in mountain,
have nothing to do but pulse
and wait
and know that I am a product of this—
we all are, all spun off in our own directions
with our own pace of decay.

      And the world feels like those days

in spring and fall when it's warmer
than you expected—
when you stand with the light and air
on closed eyelids,
and you can't tell if things are being
born or dying.

The Dying Emperor

Two daughters sit in yellow gowns at his feet,
a sleeping lamb sedate in the corner, the slaughtered pig
bleeding on the table. One daughter brought oranges
to feed his body, the other, gold to adorn it—
trinkets and relics. His blood has clotted
and belly extended.

Two watching waxen dolls—
the ash sifts around their ankles and colors
their cheekbones, flecks of fire
catch their eyes, betraying this practiced stillness,
watching him evaporate into a pile
of white birch limbs, inhaling
his inflamed breaths, wondering
exactly when the night bell will call.

External Force

Lazarus's Alarm Clock

Her skin still thick with bed heat, mouth tacky,
stomach empty, bladder pressured, brain creaking
one thought to the next and the day stretching out before,
she wants only to climb back
into bed, wants only to fall again, to sink, to float
her way down into nothingness.

Each night we die, and she likes it.

The resurrection, heralded not by angel's trumpet
and heaven's crack across the sky, but by blaring
electronic buzzing, angry sound of the color orange.
That is what says *Rise Lazarus* every morning, jamming light
back into her brain, flood of data and sensation.

Such a mean way to resurrect from the dead.

It's doubtful Lazarus's rising was a slow and luxurious lifting
out of the dark like Saturday morning, someone
rubbing your back until you rejoin the world.
No, he was jarred awake like early Monday
after a weekend of bitter arguments or a hog killing,
or late night fucking followed by insomniatic regret.

And Lazarus, buoyant out in the unworld, jarred awake,

life a stinging sizzle back into his cells, a flaring panic.
Maybe his first thought was *No, not yet,*
heart racing with shock.
Maybe Lazarus was stepping into Paradise when yanked back
to this world of pain and lies, beauty and sickness,
hunger and light, away from undone, Nothingness,

and made, yet again, to be Something.

To Speak So They Can Hear You

We gather in a room and take turns at the podium
but no one is listening.
We are all just waiting for our turn.

This is why we must believe in god.
This is why we must end up talking with our bodies—

fists crashing into eye sockets, tongues slipping across thighs.
Those are heard. Those are received.
There is very little that can be misunderstood.

When I step toward you and you step away,
that is honest. That is clear.

Things We Should Chart the Energy of

Steam in the mouth while eating hot bread.

The weight of empty work boots.

The disappointment in the sighs of Midwestern housewives.

That man's smile when looking up at the mountain snow.

Naps after sex.

Fever dreams.

Fading tattoos of devils and angels.

Scars from bicycle crashes.

Tequila.

Tequila-fed rage.

Empty wallets.

Cinnamon.

A pound gained and a pound lost.

That kiss when he finally comes back.

The old, old crabapple tree each winter solstice.

Shadows upstream and shadows downstream.

My hand on his chest at daybreak.

Erythrophobia

—fear of blushing

The thin skin
betrays, parading
the secret flare,
the denied arching
toward.
Inflammation outright.
Tiny dilation enough
to condemn,
to bring down
an empire.

Eating Flowers

The day I found you standing there, blood on your monster claws—

I hold that in the same place I hold
you dancing in the kitchen to Persian drums,
the same place I hold you
sprinkling violets from the yard on our salad.

Night Falls on the House of Animals

The breathing regular under night's navy curtain,
    like creaking ship ropes at hightide
and the lies of it
    to touch, to not touch.

This heavy sleeping hand finds a breast,
    a nipple,
windows hold out night's roar—
    even asleep the body thinks of coupling.

Knees soften and dissolve under the gurgle
    of chemicals running in red arteries,
washing the retinas, thick and dreaming,
    washing the eardrum as it rests and still absorbs,

washing the underside of acres of skin
    and priming for the hiss
of dawn's reanimation, the unstoppable desire
    to hunt and to feed.

Encountering the Only

*—Adam Rainer is the only on record
to have been both a dwarf and a giant.*

*Can you imagine, 21 and shorter
than a tomato bush?
My feet were smaller than a biscuit.
4 feet, 0 inches tall.*

*I believed in prayer
and lit the engraved candles:
Desire and Limitation.*

My daydreams follow me. Quite like a ribbon of bells tied to my foot.

I can untie the ribbon, hang the bells on the wall,
but can't ignore when they begin to shake.

*I asked god, and then thanked him,
when it began,
the pushing in my bones, the tight pulling
at my skin. Pain was tolerable.
Once I could touch the top of the window,
I felt like a man.*

I heard on TV once: "Sometimes having is not so pleasing a thing
as *wanting*. It is not logical, but is often true."

*But the screaming upward
didn't stop. I couldn't lift my monster shoes,
muscles too thin to hold a spoon,*

*and was almost 8 feet a decade later.
Can you imagine being such a man? One
who can't bend or walk himself
out to the shade trees?*

But water to a parched body…
how could that be less pleasing than suffering with those bells?

*And it won't stop. I only watch the sky cloud
and clear from my bed.*

*How could I have known
a person could pray too hard?*

Watching the mouth across the room—
the desire to be drawn in, swallowed whole,
stepping over the teeth like a garden gate, to where it stops:

spinning that worn ring around and around and around in its groove.

Caul

I know I've said before those veins
look like scrimshaw, delicate etching
on your thin eyelids. When your face
is close, nosebreath tickling my lashes,
I dream. I pinch those lids and pluck them off—
a quick popping sound, press them like bloody stickers
or kisses or welts to my cheek and watch
your staring bald eyes roll and glare.
I'll drip precious saltwater on them, keep them
taut and fresh, plump, that pale pale green
pale against your cheek as your eyelid kisses
dry into flakes and sift off.
I just want you to look at me
and now you can't roll them up
and closed, tired, slipping elsewhere.
Now like a half-fleshed bug-eyed skull you can't help
but see all I put in front of you, my square face
inches from yours, my peeling lips, my me-ness,
a demanded recognition, bulged eyes bloodshotting with vision,
unblinked attention—and I'll be there, breathing,
basking in it as those pale green planets
roll over and over me.

Ghost Dad Sings Birdcalls

We sit on Log Rock, natural sandstone bridge
spanning empty space and treetops.
He sits forward, feet swinging a little as I speak.

"I'm going to scatter some of your ashes here."

The warm breeze pushes at our backs.
A silver skipper caterpillar begins climbing his hand,
a bobble and crawl across his skin.

"I love the call of the white-throated sparrow," he says
and the skipper begins up his arm,
giant orange eyes searching for locust leaves.

I pick lichen from the rock.
"Only know the ones that introduce themselves, chickadee, whip-poor-will,
common ones like crow, grackle, mourning dove."

He returns the skipper to the rock, pointed back for the trees.
"Those are all the sad ones."
And he cleans his glasses on his shirt.
"Just make a story."

White throated sparrow says Poor   Sam   Peabody-peabody-peabody

Carolina wren is mum's favorite: *tea-kettle-tea-kettle-tea-kettle*
Olive-sided flycatcher is a drunk: *hic three beers   hic three beers*

Chestnut-sided warbler tells us to *see-see-see-see-Miss-Beech-er   see-see-Miss-Beech-er*
And Magnolia warbler calls for *pretty-pretty-Rachel,   pretty-pretty-Rachel.*"

He quiets and the air flares with birdcalls,
awareness an auditory spotlight.
Behind their songs, the forest rustles with wind, leaf-fall, twig-snap.

I hear the *Poor   Sam   Peabody-Peabody-Peabod*y of the sparrow,
the little bird lamenting to the woods over and over
that man's eternal, pitiable condition,
whatever it may be.

Acceleration

Athena to Zeus

I know you will not strike me down
because I am a favored daughter.
You split my body open, watched

the untamed horses run, and closed
it back together, seemingly whole
to the world just as my mother was

seemingly whole when you swallowed her,
heavy with child, with me. Your grand,
white, sparkling mouth hinged open

like the cracking of the earth, orange
spitting up from the base of your gut
and you pinched her by the tuft

of gown, dangled her above your white
mouth like a fat shrimp, a screaming fig
clutching desperately at her ripe middle.

I imagine you held her there,
threatening, just to prolong the terror,
your hunger, the sweet anticipation of it all,

and just as hope set in that this was another
bored game, a sandal falling and bouncing off
that pointed chin, just as she unclutched

from her belly, I imagine you glinted a little
before tossing her back, her
slipping into the bubbling red of you.

And with the ripping of a thundercurtain
I erupted from your head, completely you.
Selfish, glorious, and cruel.

Aerophobia

—the fear of swallowing air

Swallow the breath expelled by a dying mother, that last
    whisper asking where her long-dead son is.

Swallow the sound of a hand
    across the sheet of an empty bed.

Swallow the creak of the church floor, how it
    grates against the spine of the confessing.

Swallow the fights about money, the *I'll love you forevers,*
    the sudden growl of disgust, the incessant static of asthma.

Your mind bloats with visions of the Hindenburg,
    skeletal, falling, and aflame,

destroyed simply by being filled
    with poisoned air.

Hog Killing in Deep Snow

I.
The blue sky is scalding, setting the white
snow into a glare. It's going to be 10 below
and the hog will freeze to death—
18 months of investment in her 340 pounds at stake.

Bundled, the man and woman stand by the gate.
He has the pistol loaded, knives sharpened.
She has the house fire stoked and the children
packed into rainbow snow gear
so they can watch and run off to play as they wish.
They always want to watch, so eager to witness
mortality, to be able to stand back and proclaim
like the 6 year-old *She has a lot of nerves*
as the hog kicks and bleeds out onto the white.

We all watch to see that moment.

The hog eats a constellation of corn from the blinding ground.

He positions the gun above her 3rd eye, if hogs have chakras.
It's never enjoyable.
I dread this lifts into the valley's air,
followed by a loud snap and a thud.

The woman takes the pistol, hands him the blade
and purple erupts from the silent and kicking hog's neck.
Same as always.

The man tucks the burden of another animal's death into his heart.

Snow is thrown red, rolled pink as she kicks,
old lady poppy-print bedspread,
spaghetti sauce spatters on the linoleum,
purple thunderheads rolling over the field.

And a flash of lightening.
And silence.

II.
She left a smooth track arching through the snow
as they dragged her with the truck.

She left little red spots on the white
like fairytale bread crumbs.

III.
They skin the pig, pull the loose
edge and with the curved blades,
just whisper through the fat,
the muscle and the dotted underside of the hide
like gutters to bounce between,
lanes on a freeway,
ruts in the mud,
armrests at a movie theater.

The man and the woman listen to the kids
bouncing on the trampoline in their snowpants
as they undress the hog, easing her
stroke by stoke out of her own skin,
filling the air they're breathing with the heat
she had created and held at her core.

IV.
The sun slinks back over the mountain,
shadows lean blue across the snow,
gray in the last prints she left in the field,
her last walk to the gate where the dark splashes
are sinking through the white toward the frozen soil.

The hog lays on her back in the snow.
The woman puts her boot on the hog's jaw,
leans it back to expose the neck,
and begins to saw off the head.

V.
The kids want to see the heart, the bright pink spongy lungs.
They stop a snowball fight to see the guts, the aurora borealis let loose
into the wheelbarrow, shifting purples and greens, steaming.

The man and woman take off their coats and work in sweatshirts.
She is almost not a hog anymore, hung now from her feet
on the gambrel, no head, no skin, empty cage of bones and muscle,
the blood nothing but pink ice under boot.
He takes the jigsaw down her spine and the two halves
swing loose of each other, window shutters banging in a storm.

VI.
The woman lifts the back leg and he saws off the foot.
It falls to the ground,
a dropped shoe,

a teddy bear slipped from a sleeping child's arm
while carried to bed.

The woman hugs the hog's skinless leg to her chest.
The man saws the hip joint.
The hip gives and the woman catches the leg,
split firewood tumbling to the side after the ax stroke,

a block of cliff rock breaking off,
succumbing to gravity, falling free,
a ham now,
no longer a leg.

The hog dismantles.

The space the body hung in empties piece by piece,
the freezer filling with parts.
The dark migrates into the valley,
cloaks over the signs of what happened that day.
The man and woman go to bed,
aching from their work, planning the liver pâté,
the Andouille, the leaf lard in pie crusts, sausages,
ham cut and fed to people they love
on a random Sunday,
leaving the skin laying out for the chickens
to pick the fat from in the morning,

planning how to put it all to use,

everyone understanding
what decisions actually mean.

I Touched My Father's Ashes

On the dresser, in a floral box, in a clear plastic bag, I see them
for the first time. Just a pile of white,
still, and polite. They are heavy.

I poke at the bag and feel a small hard thin flake of bone.
My nail pushes into it and it breaks. The snap of that break
travels up my arm and settles in the elbow. I suddenly feel sick.

I touch the ash dusting the lip of the plastic
and streak particles across my cheeks
like war paint. I open the bag and put my hand all the way in.

It is bottomless. My elbow and shoulder slip into it,
my head dives in, legs toward the ceiling and disappearing,
being swallowed by the ash. Everything is white and muffled

and close, like a fevered blanket. The flakes,
the crumbs, like numb velvet sand,
the fragments, the ash

the ash
and there is no sound, not even
the blood in my own ears

the ash
there is one molecule of kidney,
there is one of his blonde hair

the slight curl of it vanished,
there, between those two non-things,
the pastry recipe,

his broken finger, there his anger,
the wide liver,
there his love of color,

here is the non-collection,
nothing what is was, not
recognizable as anything but quiet white.

Images for Grief

Bread with too much salt, nearly inedible.

Drought dragging on for years. The soil shrinks
and people eventually have to move away.

Picking up a glossy apple and your thumb
sinks into rot and mush.

The neighbor's pissant dog that barks non-stop
for hours at nothing while you try to sleep.

The colorblind watching a sunset.

Discovering, because they never grow in spring,
moles ate all the tulip bulbs you planted.

A mother lying to her kid so she can go out
into the rainy night to get high.

A tickle on the skin while you rock in the hammock.
When you reach for it, the yellow jacket stings deep.

Endless gravity.

The hillside slumps over years, fences leaning
at odd angles and trees trying to right themselves.

At best, a just-slightly-too-cold bath you sit in but cannot relax.

At worst, driving around a curve upon a felled tree,
crashing through the windshield head first, flying,
and body skidding across the road where all we can do
is lie there and be broken.

Momentum

The Women's Gown

Creased linen hangs on me,
generations old, under which
grandmother and mother swelled
and split and shrank with lineage,
fabric faded as fieldstones holding
me in the body.

Flames crown my head,
lick at the air, a dance
of oxygen and plasma,
uncontrollable.
I dream of evaporating,
particles spreading, disconnecting
and saying good-bye
to each other, yielding
to air currents and whatever
may come next.

But the linen keeps my molecules
bonded, a shell in which
I incubate and spin, a holy
robe that keeps me
from the sin of pride.

We Don't Waste Flat Land on the Dead

Instead we stand down on the road,
graveled and swinging with the curve of the mountain,
and we look up. Often, we squint.

We look up at death, the headstones
perched on the hill above us
like hawks, sharp eyes surveying the living.

You have the sense those hawks might,
in a noisy mess of wings and feathers, take flight
to fight or breed, but they don't. They only sit and watch.

The dead are kept up and away
from the daily movements, the biscuits and coffee,
the children's homework assignments,

the bickering of spouses, away from the television,
the laundry being folded, sex groans, and Christmas presents.
Death is up on the hill. Not here,

though something to aspire to, a mighty trek
we will all take one day, carried up that slope by someone else
as we lie back in a shiny box.

When the plastic grocery bags
the rushing floodwater snagged in the trees
on the river bank finally hang shredded

and fluttering in the air around us,
down here on the flat land of the living,
all we will see are ghosts.

What She Cannot Lay Down

The solid yellow line and the dashed white, margins to the day
stretched down the hitching ribbon. This movement never calms.

Watching one of them sit on the couch, drunk by noon and flailing
a stick through the air: the shrinking into the pit of a rotten fruit.

That roaring fuel of sins tucked brightly in the other, folded
sweetly into Oolong tea that sits just so on the bone saucer.

And of course, the sick green creeping into a body, twists and pangs
slime the tongue. Pinch the thin neck skin to test its buoyancy.

A death swells. They walk around, answer the phone,
microwave things until it's over, then wrap the corpse in newsprint.

I wish to lay her down in the dry garden where I plant my dead,
the fingers of the strange boy uncurling like a fern against her jaw.

I wish I could still the convection, that self-perpetuated upswell. The ether
unstirring would leave her alone, an empty charred husk in the quiet.

Epithalamium

I.
The ivy has taken a decade
to swallow this house, a stubborn green
fur over everything,
a hoarfrost shifting in the wind.
Its fingers peck across the cinderblock and climb,
searching for that sudden
platform of windowsill, dropping leaves
behind it like footprints,
searching for a crack, a slow-motion caress
of paint and glass.

Its prodding finger will slip
into a space in the seal of that window
and burrow in, finding the damp air
of the basement.
If you leave it alone,
the ivy will begin to vein the cluttered walls
like tributaries, one tiny thrust at a time
into the immobile dark.

II.
The daughter kneels by a school project
blanketing the mother's knees.
The mother is helping the daughter cut red and blue letters,
using the glue gun and macaroni for decoration.
They both watch the father's back, a beige cable-knit back,
answer the door. The daughter and the mother
hear a voice swell and churn like coffee rising in the pot,
then pitched wails and the dull thump of fists
against his cable-knit. The daughter and the mother
both recognize the frantic voice through its crying,
and ignore the screaming mistress on the porch.

III.
After two decades, two children grown, gardens
and broken dishes, they marry.
No one is invited.
If you ask, neither remembers the date.
Only that the minister said to the groom,
And there's my favorite motherfucking atheist.

IV.
A crabapple, bitter
and determined as a newborn's heart,

falls from the tree, its stem giving up
the struggle with gravity.
It lands in a crack on a sidewalk,
sits in a puddle when the rain comes,
dimples and molds into a brown smear.
You'd never know that smear once held
the potential to grow a tree
big enough to hold lovers in its branches.
And I wish the stem
had never bent and let the earth's pull
pluck its fruit. But then,
I would be wishing the red stone had never swelled at all,
wishing that the pink flower
had never opened to the fumbling bee,
that the entire tree had never cracked open
from its own seed in the dirt,
crabapple there by its own chance.
I'd be wishing
to undo the history of this yard, this world,
unravel the forces of creation
and evolution, be wishing to fold the galaxy,
the green burning stars,
the blue sparks of comets, the involuntary
expansion and sliding edges of this universe
back into its tiny vibrating molecule stone,
hanging from who knows what branch.

V.
The photograph is browning from the lazy arc
of sunlight that sweeps its frame each day.

The mother was younger, black hair in her eyes, toes in sand.
The father is caught in a stride of flexibility, back and knees strong.

The kid is caught in mid-swing, each hand in one of theirs, tiny feet raised
against the ocean sky like two birds aloft with the faith they will not fall.

Nephophobia

—fear of clouds

A man once lived who would lie back on a cliff and unmake clouds.
The rock would hold his back and the sky would blanket him,

the thought beginning in his solar plexus and beaming upward
into the vapor, his sheer will making the cloud vanish—

not dry it out or burn it up, not like an eraser scrubbing away
the droplets– more basic than that,

more like just unmaking it, being completely assured that there
simply was *an empty sky*, and that made it true.

It un-clouded the space, air rushing into the sudden vacancy.
And imagine a woman deciding to be loved by that man.

Instead of his body laid out on a cliff edge in the wildly un-do-able air,
he lived in a house with a toaster oven and cans of Spaghetti-O's.

Imagine how she watched his face as his gaze was drawn
out through the window pane toward the sky.

Imagine how heavy her head on his chest, that portal
where his decision left his body and changed the world.

Imagine how he closed his eyes.

Hospice

I. The First Visit
The orange lights along the drive glow
like ghosts in the night.
This is it.
Room 107.
The room in which the rainbow dragon
will curl up his tail and vanish into a cloud of wax and smoke.
We carry buckets in with us to collect any sloughed-off
iridescent scales. We will glue them
to our fingernails, tie them into our wild hair,
boil them into ceremonial broth.

The dragon sits,
and we sit, our buckets in our lap.

II. The Dash
Cell phones beckon them
like monks bell-tolling to prayer.
They bring photos of him as a child,
winter hats and scarves, temporary things
like flowers and raisins and kisses.
They come from all moments on the time-line dash
that follows his birth and will span
until that date of his death.

Daughters pace and cry.
Sons smoke and hold their babies in their arms.
Old friends study the quilt on the wall.
Summer has yielded to a late autumn
and he smiles at each one of us.

The children run outside to feed the ducks.

III. Halloween
On this night of masks, he tells his last story.
He says the chaplain who prayed over him
on his last day in ICU was praying because
he was taught it was a good thing to do,
even for a dying atheist.
We hover around the white bed, warming our hands at its heat.
He pauses a lot.

We listen.
He tells of an email from a friend that said
Last Warning.
Signed, God.

Closing out next week, we bake our doughing selves
in laughter, heralding this eminent passing
by burning sugar in our cells, unabashed.

IV. First Week in November
A baby, bare of her ladybug costume knows
there is a picture of a bunny on a wall nearby.
She knows there are fish and a brown dog living here.
She knows there is a cup of spoons in his room.
Her mother cries when she calls him pop-pop
for the first time to his non-hearing ears.

Cups of tea fall into laps and heat is passed
from small body to tie-dye teddy bear.

Motionless, we watch autumn
blaze for him, we watch the *Get Well* and
Don't be Afraid, This is a Glorious Journey cards
hang breathless on the wall.

V. Monday, November 5th
The sun rises on the dying, leaning
through slats to lie across
their yellowing bodies. Stomachs
reject breakfast, mouths open
for pain relief, a hand points at the toddler
running with the yarn scissors.

I smooth his blankets,
kiss his head,
marvel at his rolling eyes.

And while the sun sets, a gate is opening,
a bleeding, meaty gate.
As the moon gravitates into view
and the stars pock the black,
his granddaughter gives birth to a small pink boy,
moonlight silver and cool on our cheeks.

I smooth his blankets,
kiss his head,
marvel at his rolling eyes.

Never before in a day have I seen
both ends of life's spectrum.
And I can't sleep now for it.

VI. The Poised Spectators
Today's probably the day, the long-haired nurse says,
tomorrow at the latest.
The dragon's wings are moth-eaten, his breath run cold.
How do you decide what to do on a day you hear those words?
The full moon will show at high noon, shadows
will stop following us and hover in an empty bedroom.
We will drink coffee and drink coffee and drink coffee.
The seagulls will drop their white feathers,
crows their black, hawks their red tails and all will sit
naked in the cold waiting for the happy ghost
to cover them with rainbows and escort them
over the lip of the horizon.

VII. The Last Visit
It happened just as anyone could have guessed, just an old body
deciding not to breathe in again, the two women in the room,
daughters driving down roads, sons sleeping.

Then the collection began. We collected the cards
off the wall, the balls of yarn from the windowsill.
We collected the tears from each other's cheeks with our shoulders
and the salt crystals off his forehead with our lips.
We caught his dissipating fever-heat with our cold hands
and pressed it into our pockets.
The name tag on his door went into a purse,
one of his death-bed teddy bears went home with a tired baby,
his clothes went uselessly into a bag marked *Patient's Belongings*.
And that was that.

They collected him in a burgundy bag, kept him
out of the chill with a quilt and we pall bearers stood on the sidewalk
as the nurses hid around the corner to smoke,
and he went into a van and out of our sight, down the drive
lined by those orange lights that glow like ghosts in the dark.
There was nothing magical. Just broken, raw hearts
standing on a sidewalk as he went away.

Equal & Opposite Reaction

Last To-Do Lists

Abe Lincoln
1. Fire the gardener
2. Cardio 30 mins
3. Date night with Mary: *Our American Cousin*

Princess Diana
1. Call about Topeka trip
2. Burn diary
3. Harry's ear drops

Dad
1.
2.
3.

Joan of Arc
1. Find missing shoe
2. Buy cat food
3. Haircut—2:00

Rich
1. Write letter
2. Say goodbye
3. Park

Gandhi
1. Breathe in.
2. Breathe out.
3. Mail Don's birthday card.

Eve
1. Flowers to Abel's grave
2. Put away laundry
3. Find and kill that fucking snake

Me
1. Reschedule loan payment
2. Learn to blink
3. Find something to put in locket

Ghost Dad Goes Antique Shopping With Me

The cramped store smells of spiced apples—
hopeful shopkeep trying to cover dust and mothballs.

Dissatisfaction and boredom blanket his face.
I graze my eyes over the shelves of kitchen items—
rusted cast iron, a black Mammie cookie jar with a chipped red apron,
boxes of paprika, dish soap flakes,
lard, tobacco, baking powder.

He is looking at a small pair of women's shoes sitting on a bureau,
heel and sole worn, little swirls of hammer work faded
where the leather bent.
He shivers, smiles wide to make light of it.

"Too many dead people in here."

He steps to a box labeled *Instant Ancestors* and plucks the first two photos.
"See here, dated 1909. Whose baby is this?"
the pale-eyed infant stares at me, stained in sepia.

"And here." He thrusts an unhappy couple
at me. The man in the dark suit and dark beard standing
next to a woman with a lace shawl and tiny glasses.
They stand before a mill waterwheel.

"Who the hell are they? And who the hell cares?
No one cares."

He tosses the photo cards back in the box
and walks to the wall of tools, old rasps,
files, saws, mallets.

I stand next to him, look at the rusted teeth
of a 6 ft. cross cut saw, the kind two men would pull back and forth
to cut through a tree.

"Some people like to know those things
about their family history," I say to his back.

"People only need to know their own history.
And not even all of that. No need to bugger
with everyone else's."

He picks up a ball pein hammer, drops it in my hand.
The leather wrapping the handle is dry and brittle.

"Let's buy this," and he tries on old lady feather hats
to make me laugh.

But, the weight of the hammer
feels alive enough to me.

Dam

The flood happened so gradually
we just learned to walk home
the other way.

Everything was water.

Dreams about dolphins
meant we were unoriginal
and liars.

Handprints of white flour
on her navy blue apron looked
like squid.

Besides, what are the whispers of the cloistered worth?

The paperboy
on his bicycle
seemed so grown up.

And the sorrow we carry
can be mathematically figured.

Ossified

Our bones are without creed, or sex appeal,
color, or wealth, or orientation.
Our bones are the universal, the armature
on which all our dividedness hangs.

They are our map, the truth of where we come from,
where we are going. They are better teachers
than the Word of god, better to navigate by than the stars.

She laughs that when he dies, she will keep his wide span
of ribcage to make a dog house. He laughs
that when she dies he will keep her long femurs
to threaten neighborhood boys wanting to date their daughters.

The truth is, they are scared of death.
Scared not necessarily of what comes after
or what will be missed in the soap opera of the living,

but rather, afraid that they will be happy to be dead,
happy to shuck off their skin and tendons and meat
like a taffeta prom dress on a cheap hotel room floor,
happy to lay down their bones next to each other,

rib cages snagging together like Slinkys,
impossible to untangle, toe bones and finger bones clattering
into a domino pile, skulls rolling away from their necks

and telling each other stories as the teeth fall out and away
like dandelion seed fluff in the wind
when a child gasps in a breath and makes a wish.

www.ingramcontent.com/pod-product-compliance
Lightning Source LLC
LaVergne TN
LVHW041551070426
835507LV00011B/1035